Copyright © 2024 Tequila Smith.
Illustrations copyright © 2024 Shizu

All rights reserved. No part of this book may be reproduced or transmitted in any form or by any means, electronic or mechanical, including photocopying, recording, or by any information storage and retrieval system, without written permission from the author, Tequila Smith.

For information, address Ignited Ink 717 LLC, IgnitedInk717@gmail.com
www.IgnitedInk717.com

Tequila Smith is available for keynotes, panels, book talks, and workshops.

Discounts for bulk purchases of 25 books or more are available.
Visit IgnitedInk717.com to learn more and place an order.
For reprint permission, write to IgnitedInk717@gmail.com
Library of Congress Control Number: Proof

ISBN, print:979-8-9909403-0-7
ISBN, ebook: Proof
Printed in the United States of America

Dedication

I dedicate this book to my beautiful children, Tristin, Khalil, Jordan, Jaydah, and Madison. You are my heart in human form. To my mother and best friend, Gwendolyn, and my stepdad, Willie; I am forever grateful for both of you. Thank you for your love and continuous support. I aspire to make you proud. To my husband, Chris; thank you for showing me what true love is.

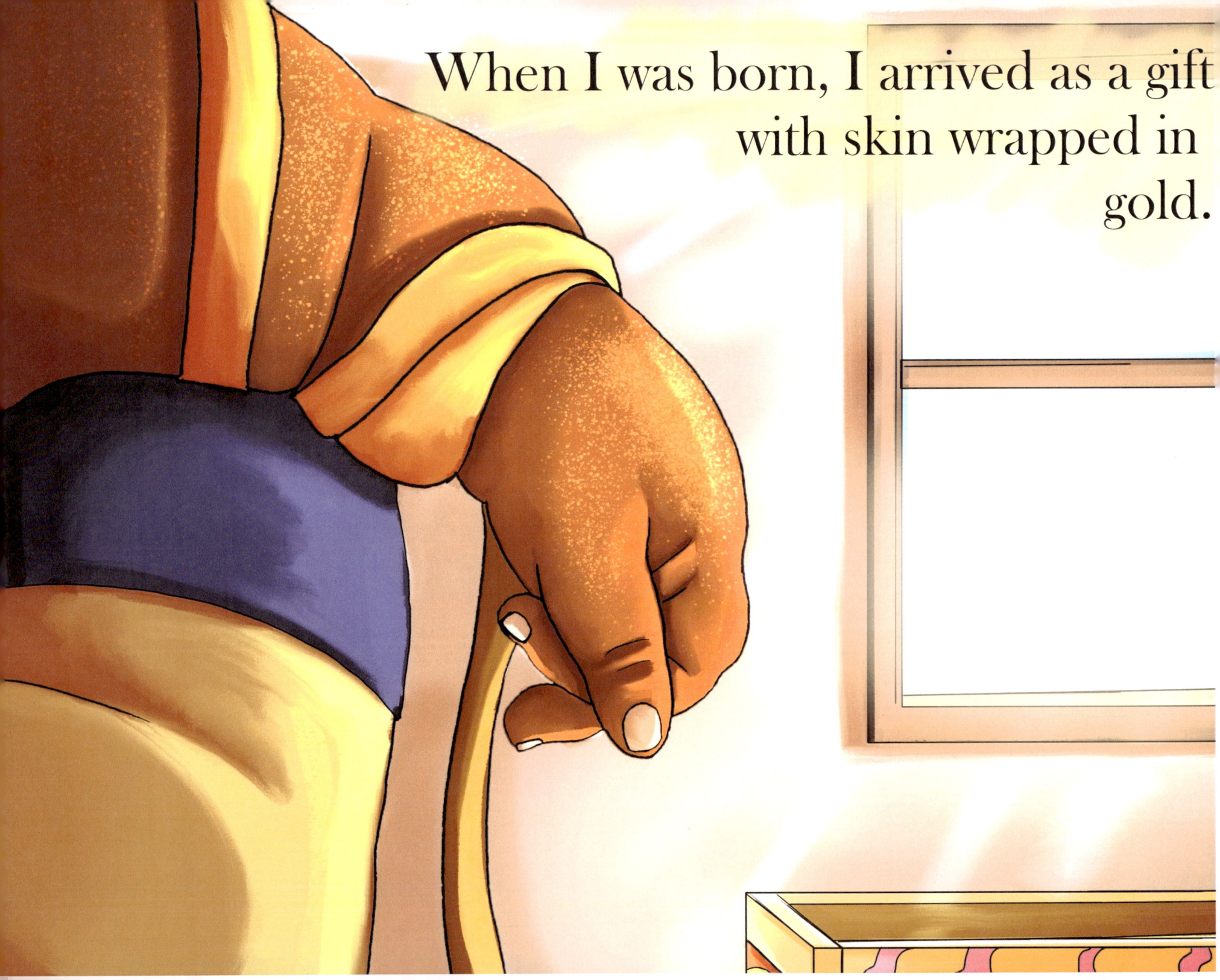
When I was born, I arrived as a gift with skin wrapped in gold.

The doctor and nurses, Mama and Daddy all beamed at my luminous glow.

As I grew, mama told me to be proud of
who I am and the package I'm wrapped in.
It is a gift. It is golden.
It- is— my skin.

I am Gifted
I am Outstanding
I am Loved
I am Dazzling

So, I remind myself every day that
I am beautiful and unique from my hair,
that I wear like a crown,
down to the tippy toes of my feet.

"It's what's on the inside that will always shine through," said Daddy.

"Be a leader. Be kind. Be loving. Treat others how you want them to treat you."

So, I practice every day to be the brightest that I can be. Shining light into darkness with love and positivity.

I show care and concern by helping others selflessly.

If everyone were the same,
what a boring world it would be.

I accept everyone for who they are and everywhere they've been.

I encourage others to embrace who they are and the beauty they see because there's only one you like there's only one me.

Everyone is special, unique in our own way,
and we should be proud of who we are each and every day.

About the Author

Wrapped in Gold was inspired by Tequila's personal struggle as a child to embrace her physical beauty. Tequila wanted to provide inspiration to other children silently struggling to accept their individual differences as beautiful, highly favored, and divinely chosen.

Tequila Smith is an Instructional Coordinator with prior teaching experience at the elementary and middle school level. She has been in the field of education for nine years. She continues to construct learning experiences that provide children of all ages with the information and confidence they need to succeed.